WHEEL OF EMOTIONS

A COLLECTION OF POETRY

ASHMIT RAJ

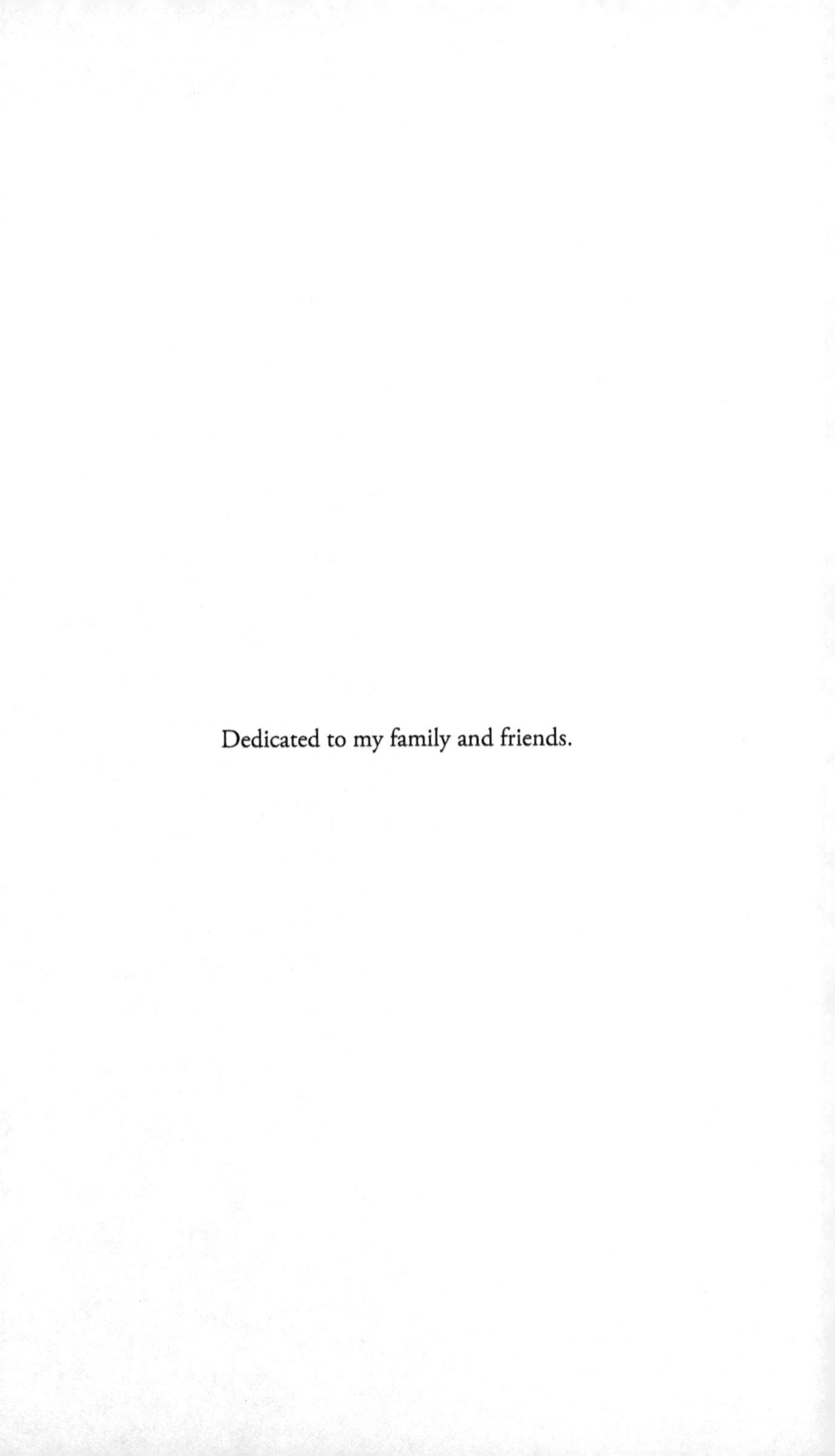

Dedicated to my family and friends.

Contents

Contents

Prologue

Emotions can be confusing! And so is life! But to make things simpler, if we can breakdown the whole of our lives in one day at a time, can't we also classify our lives into a wheel of emotions?

Plutchik's Wheel Of Emotions

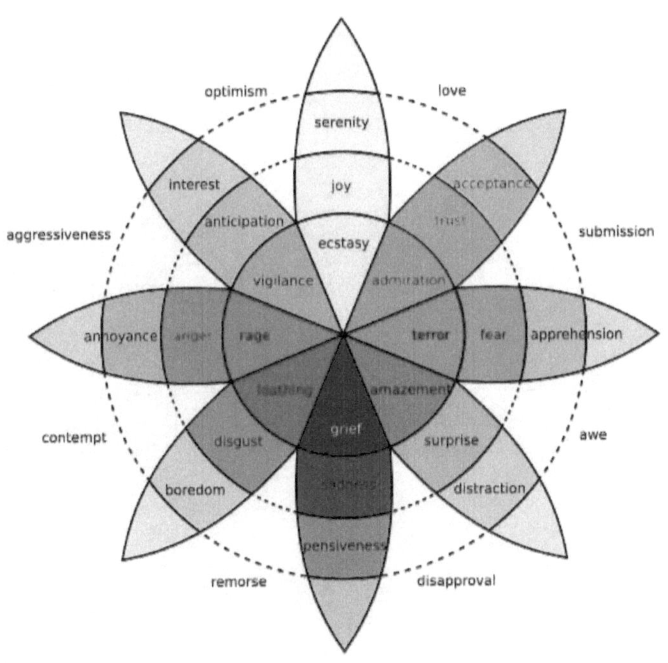

Preface

What is life?

Is it a combination of memories? A collection of bad and good experiences? A celebration? Or an accident? Each and everyone of us breathe same air and yet for each and every one of us, the meaning of life is different. This book represents life and I see life as a wheel of emotions which keeps rotating.

Emotions can be confusing! And so is life! But if we can breakdown the whole of our lives in one day at a time, we can also classify our lives into a different section or phase of emotions which come and pass us by in a second and all we can do is experience that phase and learn from it to experience even more experiences that are planted by god for us to face.

Psychologist Robert Plutchik created the Plutchik Model shown. It shows there are 8 basic emotions: joy, trust, fear, surprise, sadness, anticipation, anger, and disgust. Plutchik's wheel of emotions organizes these 8 basic emotions based on the physiological purpose of each.

But to me, this wheel of emotions starts to make sense only after I imagine it to rotate. When it starts rotating, the different emotions blend together and when they blend together, we feel them accordingly. Once, we feel the emotion above on the wheel and just after a while, when it rotates, we feel the emotion opposite to it. Isn't this life? One emotion ends when another one takes over.

Joy is the opposite of sadness.

Fear is the opposite of anger.

Anticipation is the opposite of surprise.

Disgust is the opposite of trust.

We feel joy when sadness ends. We feel fear when anger ends. And this is how the wheel of emotions work in life.

But why am I blabbering about life, emotions and this wheel of emotions here in the preface of this book and how are they related to each other? What if I say all of these are one single thing?

This book has poems which I wrote when I was at the different stages of my life where the position of the wheel of emotions was different each and every time. Every write up in this collection represents a different story and emotion. And I think that the great thing about this book and the wheel of emotions is, when you read the poems written in this book, you might also be able to connect with it by nostalgically remembering how the wheel of your emotions came to find you drowned in the emotion in which the poem you are reading was written.

I hope you enjoy this book and understand the different emotions of life through this book. Enjoy!

Acknowledgements

This book is just an outcome of the different experiences I faced and how I felt when those experiences touched me. So, I would really like to express my gratitude towards the supreme energy, god - who kept on throwing easy, challenging and interesting situations in my life so that I could feel them and make those experiences mine by writing something of my own on those experiences.

1. To art

Art. It is not just a word for me. It is a universe. It is a relationship. It is nothing and at the same time, it is everything. When you get close to your art, you start to develop a unique and beautiful relation with it. The bond between you and your art starts to grow stronger and stronger and at some point, you start talking to it like it is a human being just like you. So, here is a poem in which you will read how an artist who truly loves his art talks with it.

Every breath I breathe,
There is a mumble that goes underneath.
For the beauty on the canvas of my life you drew,
I owe so much to you.

For vanishing my tears when in need,
For cherishing them too.
For all the good you made me do,
I owe so much to you.

For all the laughs,
For dividing my heart into two halves,
For making my imaginary universe come true,
I owe so much to you.

For giving me the best of myself,

For providing me an <u>elusive</u> escape from this painful world,
For in each and every <u>indecipherable</u> situation,
providing me with help through clues,
I owe so much to you.
I don't think I'll ever break this partnership,
I don't think I'll ever be able to live without this glee,
So, you have also got some work to do.
You too owe so much to me.

elusive: rare or not easy to catch
indecipherable: not able to be read

2. Clouds go away, raindrops stay

When the hot, humid and dry surface of the earth meets cool and relaxing drops of water from up above, there is nothing but happiness around because the intense heat from which the people had been fighting earlier is now washed away. It is unreal how weather can impact the mood of a human being on such a huge scale. Rain brings many emotions with itself. So, here is a poem in which the poet has tried to explain the salubrious impact of rain on the people.

The infinite drops falling from above,
Seemed to spread nothing but love.
Through these drops,
I went on a journey to the clouds,
I felt something,
It was beyond the chaos of the crowd.
On hearing those droplets making soothing sound,
I sensed nothing but peace around.
All of the miseries vanished,
As the drops fell below.
Every negative moment passed quickly,
And the positive ones became slow.

The smell of the mud,
Produced by the water filled pits.
Made my heart beat even faster,
And I smiled with the rhythm of it.
The effect of this <u>tableau</u> on my brain,
Made me wish that on every day of the year, it rained.

tableau: a scenery

3. You know what's funny?

Sometimes, the clock doesn't tick your way and the world doesn't revolve how you want it to. Each second feels like a burden and each friend feels like an enemy. In times like these, the only true friend of an artist is his art. Likewise, a writer's true friend in his misery is a pen. Whenever a poet feels sad, he writes a poem about it and eventually feels satisfied about it if it turns out to be a good one. So, here is a poem in which the poet has poured out a valuable emotion through his ink: sadness.

You know what's funny?
My heart stays happy,
But when it's sad, it cries from its core.
You know what's funny?
There are so many pages of wishes I have tore.
You know what's funny?
I liked it better when I was four.
You know what's funny?
I have always preached about the lawlessness of false
happiness,
But the cloth of false happiness, I myself have wore.
You know what's funny?

I want to know what is wrong with the <u>delinquent</u> cosmos,
But I'm always too scared to open that door.
You know what's funny?
That it is not funny anymore.

delinquent: of a bad behaviour

4. You

Love. Love is not something to be written, talked or read about. Love is way beyond all of this. It can only be felt and each and every one of us feels it in a different way. When a person is love-struck, he becomes fanatic of the person he falls for at such a level that he forgets that it is all going to end one day; and whenever love ends, everything ends. Real heartbreaks make your heart stop working. Although, love is something that never ends, the person with whom we fall in love is not meant to be with us forever. And the inevitable thing that confirms the separation between the two lovers is death. So, here is a poem in which the poet has described an imminent end of a beautiful journey of an old couple in love.

On the pillars of shivering feet,
The building of a weary old body stood in <u>ambivalence</u>.
When he saw her heartbeat gradually decelerating, the building's pillars lost its balance.
It was just on the verge to collapse, but she smiled.
It stayed still when he saw her loose cheeks occupied for a while.
A few seconds of her duchenne smile <u>ricocheted</u> years of love.
It was not <u>privy</u> to him that it was all going to end and she'll <u>anon</u> depart above.

He smiled while vouching down to run his hands on her forehead,

Giving a soft brush of his lips to hers, "Dont worry love, I'll be good.", he said.

She breathed, he breathed, nothing was left to be said and only the eyes talked.

She lied, he stood, but with their hand in each other's hand, through the whole journey of her life they walked.

He felt the absence of her presence even before her departure,

His face was calm, but from within, he was battling a great torture.

The less she talked, the more sound the monitor made,

Hearing the monitor beeping, he wondered if their destiny was vague.

He then acknowledged the memories to which, together, they gave birth to.

Which he could cherish at that moment and even after she left the earth too.

As her breath haulted and as the beeps got deep,

He couldn't control his cry and she heard him weep.

She wanted to reach his face and she tried her best.

But she gathered all of her strength to keep her hand on his chest.

Her tenuous lips said "I love.." when her hand fell off of his chest scraping his heart like broken glass.

"You", he completed crying uncontrollably at the last.

ambivalence: confusion
ricocheted: rebound
privy: unknown
anon: soon

5. Red drop

Periods. A phase through which every girl goes once in a month. The process of menstruation is a beauty in itself but to a girl, it is much more painful and bad. The people, especially in India, are not given proper education about this topic because of the so called embarrassment and shyness. But because of this, it has become a major problem. The problem is that a majority boys do not understand about what problems and how much pain girls face during their periods and they fail to comfort them, which is their responsibility. So, here is a poem in which the poet has explained to the boys how to take care of their mother, sister, friend or any girl who are on their periods and how normal and beautiful periods actually are.

Go on a soothing date,
Buy her a chocolate,
Comfort her with your lullabies,
Hug her whenever she cries,
And when the pain starts to grow,
And the tears start to flow,
Be a man and show some care.
Give her some strength so the immense pain she can bear.
In your arms, taking a leap,

With the growing calm, she will sleep.
Saw her sleeping peacefully,
Thus, my day ended beautifully.
She met me in my dream,
Saw her eating ice cream.
It gave her a little relief from the pain,
The smile on her face while eating has been stuck in my
brain.
Sometimes, I wonder how much injustice of god this is,
But then I also realise how beautiful of a process it is.
I hope she comes out of her sleep a little relieved.
Because she is the strongest person ever, that's what I believe.

6. Price of my soul

Fear is one of the strongest feelings I have ever faced. This poem was written by me when I was battling this great emotion and it taught me how to gear up and face tough situations alone.

When I saw that volcanic eruption,

There was no one and I went forward in circumspection.

The aftermath was appalling and I was inspired by the annihilation.

The obnoxious fire led my mind to think about cold.

With my anxious nerves, my soul too was sold.

They felt priceless,

Even though they were priced less.

The hot and cold both with this sale increased by twice.

Never knew I would be affected by my own soul's price.

Never knew I would be affected by my own soul's price.

7. Incandescence of December

We all have a place or a person where we can go to and feel the safest and the most secure. Be it your roof, balcony, friend, family, relative, window or even your bedroom. We all are usually strong enough to face our problems alone but sometimes, when the situation gets out of your hand, you have no option left but to take help. In this poem, that help is the 'cold breeze'. This piece of text is a little figurative as the poet's 'cold breeze' can be anything of yours - any person or thing or nature or literally the cold breeze. So, here is a poem in which the poet has conveyed the importance of 'cold breeze' or anything that helps you when you are low.

On my roof, I stood aloof, breathing with a knife in my wind pipe.
I came to end it all. I came to put a full stop on my life.
There stood I, with shivering feet, feet above ground.
There was no one to stop me but I heard one sound.
Catching me on my own terrace like a burglar,
I was not in awe to see who was it, it was her.
I <u>abominated</u> her as she kept smiling at me, my misery and my past.
Is there anything left to see now? I asked my mind, my breath

and my heart at the last.

She replied to my thought with a cold smile.

On seeing that, I forgot my ache for a while.

She gradually became the moon to me, but I was her star.

She was an open book, even though I, <u>ajar</u>.

Her obscurity held me in her arm,

All of the <u>catastrophe</u> ended with the stroke of her palm.

She, came by and went by as if she was playing with me.

The <u>discombobulation</u> changed to hope, and the hope gave me glee.

After she calmed me down, she came to sit by my side with ease.

While she sat down; I said, "Thanks for everything, cold breeze."

abominated: hated

ajar: partially open

catastrophe: a sudden disaster

discombobulation: confusion

8. Again

The cycle of emotions keeps circling on until we die. It is the only thing that is constant. If we are happy, sadness is destined to come and conquer us and if we are sad, happiness is destined to come and conquer us; this is how it is. This is how god has made us. Although, the thing stated above is a fact, it does not really mean that we should not celebrate our happiness and sadness too. Every emotion is a gift in itself if we use it right. I channel my sadness and anger through my art. So, here is a poem which was written while celebrating pain and sadness.

Again,
I sit on a chair on which, fell a drop of my tear.
Feeling just like an infant,
Who is hesitant to go on a stage.

Again,
I have a pen among my fingers
Feeling just like a prisoner,
Stretching his hands to get out of that rotten cage.

Again,
While writing, my hands shiver.
Feeling just like an old man,
Wanting to die being fed up of his age.

Again,
I can feel the tears,
Spreading underneath my breathe.
Just like this pen is spreading ink on the page.

9. That hug

Kindness. It is a virtue that can change one's perspective towards life. It can change the whole lifestyle and even our mindset. Who knows what the other person is going through? If the other person is going through something, how bad would that person feel when he or she is treated arrogantly? Whenever we look out just for ourselves just to do our own work and accomplish our own achievements, we feel happy. But when we do good for others, help them and show them love, god feels happy. So, this is a poem in which the poet has explained the importance of kindness and the regret that comes to us later in our lives if we spend all of our lives being selfish and living just for us.

In the hot mornings of June, she used to sit alone,
I went by that street everyday, t'was infront of my home
Nobody cared for her, not even herself,
I couldn't do anything for her, even though I wanted to help.
She sat on a wheelchair as weary as her legs while the sun shone on her head,
Seeing her condition, I wondered how many days ago she might have had a bread.
"Never mind." I whispered to myself refuting the empathy that arose in me.

I went running with my bat in a <u>disparate</u> route under a tree.

"Come on now and bowl" I shouted at my friend taking stance,

I forgot the old woman, drenched in the game's trance.

Looked at her as soon as I hit the ball,

Realised that is not where I wanted to play at all.

The ball raced towards her quicker than I wanted,

My heart pounded as quickly as the ball and my heart, my mind daunted.

What I did not want, exactly that happened,

She cried out loud in ache, as if her world came to end.

I ran to her faster than the ball did,

She was crying, but seeing me, the drops of tears she hid.

"Are you okay?", I asked her hesitantly,

I sat down and seeked for her leg gently.

I could tell by her face that she was <u>irate</u>,

Still, she is okay she tried to imitate.

She told me that the previous morning, a car had hit her wheelchair and ran away.

I saw only a warm bandage wrapped around her ankle and had nothing to say.

I asked her if she had anyone to take care of her leg.

"My son." She replied. "He has gone for some money. He has gone to beg."

My friend just said sorry and went back to play.

I stood there silently, realising my lips wanted to, but had nothing to say.

Being a 10 year old unemployed boy, all I could do was give her my cap.

"God bless you my son.", she replied back.

I could sense the pain, the joy and the sadness in both of our insides.

I involuntarily sat again on my knees to hug her tight.

After that, I saw my watch and realised how much time has passed by.

I completed the hug and said to her, "Goodbye."

Next day, I did not see the woman, just the wheelchair.

My innocent mind just thought that she might have gone somewhere.

If I knew that while growing up, this memory will gradually get blur.

If I knew that it was my last goodbye to her.

I would've stayed there with her no matter how much it got late.

Because I still remember clearly that hug till date.

disparate: different
irate: angry

10. Intoxication is all I need

Intoxication is something that can either make one's life or destroy it. If one is addicted towards intoxication of a good thing like art, it will make his life awesome. On the contrary, if one is addicted towards intoxication of bad things like drugs, it will destroy his life. So, here is a poem in which the poet refers to art as his intoxication.

Intoxicate me.
Eradicate me from the afraid ones,
And blend me with all of those dusky shades.
Where the space for tears is none,
And where the false happiness is made.
Intoxicate me.
And feel sad that you intoxicated me.
I'll give you company in your sadness with the regret of intoxication in me.
Intoxicate me.
See your own reflection in my half closed eye.
And realise your lips are starting to smile,
With mine.

Intoxicate me.

But don't stay.

For if you do, you'll also start to get intoxicated too and make this night your day.

Intoxicate me.

Not with the coloured water or smokey cigar or its son.

But with art and its never abiding run.

Intoxicate me.

And I know my thoughts will start to unfold even faster.

As it is the only intoxication I don't feel guilty after.

11. Why can't a person wake up when he dies?

Death. It is the only truth that sets us free from the cycle of life: the wheel of emotions. We are generally so lost in our lives and start loving our lives so much that we start to get scared from what is eventually going to happen with us. We all are going to die one day and every breath we inhaled and exhaled are all going to be vain. So, here is a poem in which the poet has tried to say that the art we make, the relations we build, and the positivity we spread while living our lives are going to be eternal. It has a healthy discussion about death. And eventually, It also asks a question that 'why can't a person wake up when he dies?'

❧❧❧

The closing of the thousand eyes of my mind and the only eye of heart.

is now evident to the thousand eyes of nights and the only eye of day.

The inevitable shot his dart right on the target and thus, I depart.

I depart with pending goodbyes hoping to meet them in their prays.

Is this the end? Or the beginning of the time where, time I can bend?

Can I talk to my people from this side? Or is there any signal to them I could send?

Lying comfortably, I'm clueless about why they are uncomfortable.

Only the few who did not know me very well are able.

The close ones are still <u>scrupulously</u> looking at me.

My eyes are closed but their <u>ambiguous</u> look I can see.

The talks of my about my inspirational feats and brave bets,

Spread as if they have been <u>aggrandised</u> by my death.

I wanted to smile and comfort their cries,

But that a person cannot do when he dies.

Why can't the <u>desiccated</u> body wake up when it lies.

Why can't a person wake up when he dies?

scrupulously: carefully
ambiguous: having more than one possible meaning
aggrandise: to increase the power
desiccated: dried out

12. Swings

The ever increasing technological amenities have many pros but some cons too and this poem is about one of those cons - the decline of the social life of mankind. Previously, people were united because they used to meet face to face. The lack of meetings due to the ease of online conversations and the other infinite reasons are causing the swings which were once filled with joy of the innocent children and their cries to move alone with the help of chilling breezes.

On one of the swings in the night I sat.

The crispy crawling leaves sent my thoughts back.

Back in the time when the swings were more than an empty void.

Far from the online discussions of who is better, apple or android.

The time when people got physically injured and not emotionally hurt.

When not mouths but people's dresses were full of dirt.

The chilling breeze made the swings sway.

The thought of unity and humanity with the empty swings, swung away.

13. Darkness of the night sky

This is one of the figurative poems of this book. When you are all drained in the misery, you start to blame the universe. You get so lost in the blame game that you forget that the darkness lies within you and it is your responsibility to remove that darkness. So, here is a poem in which the poet likewise blames the universe but he eventually realises that the misery was in front of him the whole time and it was his responsibility to wipe the misery off.

The overwhelmed moon asked the stars to gather in space.

They did; they played the card of trump against my ace.

The decline of my <u>dexterity</u> they saw.

Wanted to scratch their shine with my claws.

God gave me darkness, and in great proportionality.

And their shine turned my <u>premonition</u> into an egregious reality.

I asked the innocuous stars why were they so cruel.

Their dimmed shine replied that it is not them, it's the moon's rule.

The steam engine of my ignorant anger suddenly came to hault.

Why am I being so arrogant to stars? Isn't it all the moon's fault?

In the night sky, I was made vulnerable to dwell.

Not to find I in darkness, but the darkness in myself.

dexterity: skilled at doing things

premonition: a feeling that something unpleasant is going to happen in the future

14. Hospital

This poem was written by me when I was in a hospital handling a great deal of pain and physical torture. There, I saw a two year old boy who was more physically challenged than me and still he was handling all that pain with great ease. How was it so that such a little kid could handle this much pain and torture so nonchalantly? What was it that made him different? And what was it that made him so strong? After giving this a serious thought, I came to a single conclusion, it was his mindset. He taught me that it doesn't matter if the torture is physical or mental, your mind plays a great role in tackling it.

A delirious thought to my broken mind came around,
When heavily dosed me on a hospital bed I found.
It asked me to close my eyes when I saw something strange.
I saw a two year old boy with infinite bandages on his head crowned.
I complained and complained about my pain,
Until I saw that boy fighting it bravely with his brain.
With his mind, his bandaged mind.
Oh what an embarrassment it was on me that rained.

15. Perfectly fine

This was originally a write up which I later composed as a song and it eventually became a part of my music album - MY DIARY. This poem is simply about the feeling of love and how pure and blissful of a feeling it is to experience.

If you're standing among thousand, there's only you in my sight.

I never knew there'd be someone, who would make my life so bright.

Whenever I see you I feel my heart and I smile with the rhythm of it.

If falling in love feels like this, I want to fall in every pit.

Just a moment of me remembering you makes me feel how fast flies the time.

Just a single thought of you makes my day perfectly fine.

Whenever I see you smiling, I feel my heart waking up.

Whenever I see you crying, I feel my heart breaking up.

Maybe we're gonna be away from each other sometimes but,

I know we'll be alright but, yes, it hurts.

No matter how many silly mistakes I make, I know you'll not mind.

No matter how many problems we face, I know well solv
them by line.
No matter how many people are behind you, just know that
you're mine.
Now just hold my hands and everything will be perfectly fine.

16. A week without phone

As beneficial as they are, mobile phones can be full of cons too. Although it depends upon how we use it, we gradually get compelled to it and at the end of the day, it becomes one of the most important things in our life and whenever we are without it, we feel incomplete. So, here is a poem which is written on how we have become totally dependent on our mobile phones and how we have been totally lost in the screens of our mobile phones.

"Be without mobile phones for a while."
Our teacher said, "You'll feel as good as one feels while walking barefooted on grass."
On hearing this, our appalled hearts broke into infinite pieces of glass.
As the first day went by,
Our hearts beated with a <u>scrupulous</u> cry.
As if they were begging for that five-inch screen.
"Only if I could chat with my friend. How good it would have been.".
I thought.
And with the <u>stupefaction</u> of mobile phone, my will power still fought.
I did not <u>deign</u> to wake up,

As the second day came up.

The loathe of the phone's absence took over my mind.

Something to distract myself, I was vulnerable to find.

As its absence was intricate,

And the strings of my mind and heart were <u>irate</u>.

Anyhow the second day had gone.

Through a <u>dessicated</u> night, the morning of the third day was born.

Woke up and immediately searched for my phone.

Was just left with an empty void as I felt like I was not at home.

Sat on the window throughout the day,

Everyone talked but I was left with nothing to say.

Within that chaotic silence, the third day went by,

"I'll do something tomorrow and be happy.", I thought to give this thought a try.

Next morning when I woke,

I realised today is the fourth.

I took one pen and a paper and drew the scene outside my window.

I couldn't draw it perfectly but I thought,

"A small win though."

Through that drawing, I got a little more positive.

The silent mouth got a little more talkative.

On day five,

I gave that drawing one more drive.

I drew well, but still <u>repudiated</u> that sheet.

I thought of my phone and whispered, "Only if I had Google to cheat."

Still, on day six I gave it a final shot.

Eventually, the stroke of perfection, my drawing caught.

I forgot my misery and my classmates.

And realised I had been without my phone for six separate dates.

My drawing reflected positivity pf the social world

And how within a five inch box the humans have been curled.

On the seventh day, I showed my drawing to my class.

I was as satisfied as one is while walking barefooted on the grass.

scrupulous: careful

stupefaction: surprise

deign: to do something although you think you are too important to do it

irate: angry

desiccated: dried out

repudiated: rejected

17. You are it.

When god takes away love from you, he takes everything from you and yet you somehow become strong. But when god gives you love, he gives you everything and yet you somehow become weak. So, here is a sonnet which introduces the readers to the vulnerability and weakness of a lover.

What expectation do I have from thee?

What the mankind has from a tree.

Why do those ticking toes stop the clock?

like the minute and hour hand has together been blocked.

The way it is getting <u>confiscated</u> from my hand.

The tragedy couldn't be anymore grand.

So, come to me, you beautiful piece of art; believe me, you are

it.

Does the revelation make you anxious?

Or have you always been so <u>precocious</u>?

Like me, who often sings melancholic tunes.

Or thee, who often carries happiness' dunes.

I call you dune but don't be sand,

On the shoulder of mine, keep your hand.

And come to me, for you don't live in my heart, you are it.

confiscated: take something from somebody as a punishment
precocious: developed certain ways of behaving at a much younger
age

18. Can I drink you?

'Can my soul drink you? Or you too are real?' Just these two lines of this poem are enough to introduce it. It was written for every valuable thing present on this earth. It was written for anything that attracts anyone. It was written in a sense of vulnerablity, misery and it was written for the people who think that they have already lost something and they cannot get over it until they find it.

They see the curtain over the mistakes and not the improvements over the curtain

A lot of me is left for them to see, I am certain.

I don't have a lot of time

For this silly clock ticks the life away

And thus I need the help of your magic

To find myself a sane path or an insane way

Can my soul drink you?

Or you too are real.

Is your artistry visible only in dreams or

Can I see it in real?

I'm scared that you'll not identify me by my condition.

But I'm sure that I'll identify you even by your single hair.

Maybe it might take a lot of effort.

Maybe for you it won't be fair.

But still, I need to drink you whether you're solid, gas or liquid.

I'll be gay still if the taste of yours is insipid.

I'm lost in the blue ocean of debts,

Or should I say, the ocean of blues.

Drinking you, there'll be no doubts left.

Drinking you, I'll clear all my dues.

19. 1 girl. 67 DNAs.

It is heartbreaking to see the rape cases becoming so common and kindness, justice and love becoming so bizarre nowadays. Each and everyday the rape cases are increasing in number and the people in power and without power both, are sleeping unaffected. So, here is a poem on a news which I read a few days back which shook me.

No one came to save her; and every man thinks of himself as if he is wearing a cape.

A girl was left unattended on the streets after getting raped.

The <u>ostentatious</u> clouds tricked us all.

They went dark and yet there was no rain at all.

They ask me what is wrong with us.

Whom to love and whom to trust.

They found an eight year girl with 67 DNAs inside her I read.

That is what is wrong with us.

ostentatious: behaving in a way that is intended to impress

20. Division of me

Sometimes it is all about not giving up and still walking in the rain of glass. You hear all of those quotes and sayings about not giving up even if the whole world is against you or the failures are the only stepping stones of your success, but there comes a point when you just cannot bear with the failures, rejections and the self doubt you come across after facing these things. So, this poem is about the doubts and thoughts you come across when you are at that point of your life.

Walked to be apart and walked in a parade.
I saw my legs moving but no <u>accolade</u>.
I had my heart but was doubtful if it beated.
To make it work, is there anyway it can be treated?
Similar questions arose with the ever walking calender.
Divided myself, Just to build a stack of questions and quotient and no remainder.
"Is he better, or a go getter?"
"Am I prepared?" And I saw the stack of my confidence shatter.
I looked up to see where it went.
Just to find a drone with a dent.

Looked like my destiny was hovering over me with that
drone.

Still, thinking of Green Day, I walked alone.

accolade: mark of acknowledgment

21. I belong here

We all have a comfort zone. A place where we shouldn't be for a long period of time, but we want to be there forever. That place hugs you without hugging you. That place talks with you without saying anything. That place introduces you with your own thoughts and that place makes you realise that you belong here in this world. So, here is a poem which is written on one of those places.

I belong here.
Losing all the practicality and the feeling of being also-ran.
I got lost in the bewildering reflection of the moon,
embedded on the surface of the river Ganga.
I was sent to a place where I shouldn't have been.
Leaving all of the deceptions behind;
And all the grudges I beheld.
The <u>exactitude</u> of the abstract was such that the water was walking and I was floating.
The street lamps of the bridge behind outshined the stars,
But couldn't outdate them.
That's when I realised that I breathe but I'm a star and the lamp doesn't but still, it is nature.
It thinks of himself as inevitable, but I have died already and

have got nothing to lose.

So, the "inevitably" right nature tells me that I shouldn't be here.

Maybe it did so for me only but I interpreted it for my own good.

And now I know that I belong here.

exactitude: the quality of being exact

22. Pessimistic sonnet

The regular tests we face in our life are the deciding factors of how we are doing in life emotionally and practically. Sometimes we pass them easily but the tests which we cannot pass easily make us doubt ourselves. Maybe the never ending series of tests taken by god is the only constant in our life. So, here is a poem which is about the tiredness you feel when you cannot catch a break from these indubitably tough tests of god.

The stress ridden me,

Is now a hidden bee.

Torn up and <u>desiccated</u>.

Not a skill and only educated.

Know how to build a nest,

Still can't, after giving my best.

When will it end? Is it a never ending test?

Or do I have to end it myself and take rest?

Is my destiny shy?

Or it, I have to buy?

Will the bought destiny be enough?

Or will it make my flesh rough?

Is it selfish to remember him only in miseries?

is it a sin to tell him that his test is <u>indubitably</u> tough?

desiccated: dried out
induvitably: without any doubt

23. Sunset

Nature. A very significant part of our life which we ignore very easily. The beautiful agents of nature - the sun, the moon, stars, the sky, the trees and every bit of air we breathe - say something different to all of us. Its just upon us whether we want to hear it or not. When we talk with nature, it tells us so much without uttering a single word. This is the power of nature. So, here is a poem which is written on thoughts I had while witnessing sunset.

The aggregation of the burning sun,
Felt <u>ambiguous</u> and relax none.
Don't know why it still felt soothing.
When what it really did was give me a burn.

A burn that left me with a scar.
A scar that set my comfort afar.
The comfort where I prospered.
The place that felt proper.
The sunlight wanted to tear my flesh out.
There was no noise of the chaos, but my eyes heard a shout.
The shout had many questions hidden behind,
The answers to which within the sunlight I dared to find.
The questions entangled my eyes with the sun even more.
"Oh, how much I love the night, how much the sun I

<u>abhor</u>."

Thought I while giving the eternal marathon of thoughts a

pause.

Among the questions that arose, one of the most interesting

was-

How is it so that there are a thousand reasons to panic,
But to calm down only one?
The aggregation of the burning sun,
Felt ambiguous and relax none.

ambiguous: having more than one possible meaning
abhor: hate

24. The line

Here in this poem, the line which is getting talked about is the line that we can wipe off and unite the world or the line that we can intensify by spreading hate among the society and watch the world burn in front of our own eyes due to our own actions. So, here is a poem that is written to open the eyes of those who are intensifying this line without even knowing.

And here I stand on the line that lies between the wrong and the right
Wondering is it the line to be darkened or the line to fight.
Rich scolding a poor double of his age;
Trapped between the pride of his wealth and his absurd rage.
The politician who promised of crime disrupt
After getting in power, got himself corrupt.
The adjunction of greed and broken promises.
The separation of logic on the absurd premises.
The exacerbating murders on the name of caste.
The ignorant present and the arrogant past.
Standing on the line, I realised a few more things.
There are a lot of lies on the table; and the truth, no one brings.
Stepped off the line and looked at it once more.

The line is being intensified and no one opens this thought's
door.
The line is present everywhere,
Doors of the rich and curtains of the poor.
Torn tents on the left.
Skyscrapers on the right.
The line among these is what we have to fight.

exacerbating: worsening

25. Dance of shadows

This poem can be about anything you love that makes you feel like the better version of yourself and that you feel is the supreme form of beauty. I personally wrote this poem on one of closest art forms to me, dance. Dance is a poem without words. It makes me feel more like myself. It makes me love myself and that is the reason I love it more than anything.

I stood still while my shadow started to move.
With the sound of footsteps of itself it started to groove.
How was it happening? because <u>intextricable</u> it was.
Knew the consequences but didn't know the cause.
The problem seemed to <u>ameliorate</u>.
And from myself, my soul started to alienate.
The shadow moved as if it was free.
It asked me to close my eyes and count to three.
One. Two. Three. And a whole different universe!
There was no chaotic noise; only the sound of a soulful verse.
The verse of the angels, which could heal any damage.
I looked and they looked not only beautiful but also savage.
Their eyes poured a drink of intoxicating movement in my eyes' purse.
All of my pay which was due to the angels, gradually started

to emburse.

Neither pain, nor the suffering and no reality was in that universe.

It didn't seem like a beautiful lie, it felt like a beautiful curse.

inextrcable: impossible to escape from
ameliorate: to make something better

26. A tale of freedom

People say that discipline gives you a better boost to work than motivation. As correct and valid as this statement is, I personally believe that motivation is underrated. This is because the boost it gives might be suffice for a short period of time, but it is enough to make one realise his or her purpose in his or her life. Motivation gives you the reason to live. It is pure. So, here is a poem which conveys that sometimes, all your rusty and tired heart needs is a little motivation.

She surmised my agitation,
And summerized my situation.
I created contrived imaginary bars,
Behind which I was left ajar.
No one came to save me.
It had been ages since I saw the brave me.
She scraped off the rust,

And wiped away the dust.
Just to discover my old version.
Scared and still, ready to burst.
It was ready to burst, ready to fly.
The imaginary bars now seemed to cry.
The old me flew away, the new me conquered the sky.

'Thanks!', the new me said to her flying by.

surmised: to guess or suppose that something is true without definitely knowing
contrived: not realistic

27. Two rains

Earlier in this book, you might have have read a poem which deciphered wonderful and positive impact rain brings on the earth. In this poem, you are going to read that a single rainfall can affect two people differently depending upon their background and condition.

❧❧❧

To increase, but to also reduce the the citizens' pain,
The evening came with the strong thunderstorm and rain.
The shopkeeper who was hopeful for the evening to come and make his shop run,
Was obligated to go to his home empty pocketed and leave his shop adjourned.
His boy and girl waited for him with stomachs just like his pocket - empty.
But if pain was measurable just like money, the man's eyes carried plenty.
As soon as he saw his kids' faces, the pain of the vulnerable shopkeeper gradually turned into a tear.
His neighbours, with half of clothes and full of joy, enjoyed bathing in the rain while the man feared.
The man cried a river while the neighbours enjoyed the heavy rain.

The family went inside to obviate the deteriorate of their health afterwards, and

The man wiped off his tears thinking that he now has nothing to lose, ignoring the fact that he had nothing to gain.

The irony that was reflected by the rain in this city that night was fantastic.

Even though it rained same on both the households, the impact on one was drastic.

The raindrops resembled the tears falling from almost everyone's eyes.

Some were crying because of happiness, but some cried melancholic cries.

28. Is it all a myth?

This poem is not a statement, it is a question. It is written in a state of doubt and in a state of wonderment. A doubt that does he really want the things which we give him in the religious places? Even though we do these things because of our faith, wouldn't he want us to give the money and things which we give to him to be given to the poor and unprivilaged ones who need help?

Is it all a myth?
Or does he really exist?
Do the problems arise because of our own characters?
Or does he really test us?
Are the temples, mosques and churches really mandatory to visit?
Or is he everywhere?
Do you really have to tell him your wishes
For him to become your hope in despair?
Does he really need the food you bought for him with even more rupees beside.
Or did he provide you with that rupee to ease the life of a beggar dying of hunger just outside.

29. Black, white & grey

When you start liking someone, you want them to know but you also don't want them to know. It is a confusing yet beautiful phase. One sided love or attraction is an experience in itself which we all have felt at least once in our life. As once the famous Indian comedian and poet Zakir Khan said, "When you are in a relationship, you win the day when the relationship starts and you lose the day when the relationship ends, but in a one sided relationship, you win every single day; you lose every single day."

I scraped his name in that star thinking no one could read it.
That star shone brighter than every other star in the sky.
Even though it was night,
his name with that star shone higher than high.

Although people didn't matter,
The less his name spread among people, the better.
Walking down the aisle with my look towards him,
While the chants of our love story people chatter.

This is all I can think about.
In my thoughts, him having all the clout.
I hope he knew what I thought,
While being with me on this journey throughout.

Oh what an ache it is to keep your mouth shut,
When you know you have got so many things to say.
The whole world is busy within the black and white,
And all you are stuck in is within the grey.

30. Wheel of emotions

Ecstacy taught me to stay grounded.

Pain taught me to keep my head up high.

Terror taught me to gather all my strength.

Rage taught me to just breathe and let everything pass by.

Surprise taught me the value of my closed ones.

Trust taught me how to make friends.

Love taught me to make efforts for them.

Annoyance taught me to make my mind go through some amends.

Confusion taught me to accept.

Acceptance taught me that its okay to be confused.

Grief taught me that everything is temporary.

Boredom taught me that my mind is vain when its fused.

All of these emotions mash up together and make life,

And it keeps the fire within us burning.

All of these emotions keep on coming and going.

And the clock constantly keeps this wheel of emotions turning.